The Forest

by Rita Crosby

Editorial Offices: Glenview, Illinois • Parsippany, New Jersey • New York, New York
Sales Offices: Needham, Massachusetts • Duluth, Georgia • Glenview, Illinois
Coppell, Texas • Sacramento, California • Mesa, Arizona

ISBN: 0-328-13172-5

7 8 9 10   V010   14 13 12 11 10 09 08

We looked around the forest.

We saw these trees and animals.

We looked around the forest.
We saw trees that grow
green leaves.

4

We looked around the forest.

We saw trees that grow

yellow leaves.

We looked around the forest.

We saw a squirrel eat a nut.

We looked around the forest.
We saw a huge bear find food
under the water.

We looked around the forest.

We saw a bird in a tree.